Colours

An Anthology of Poems

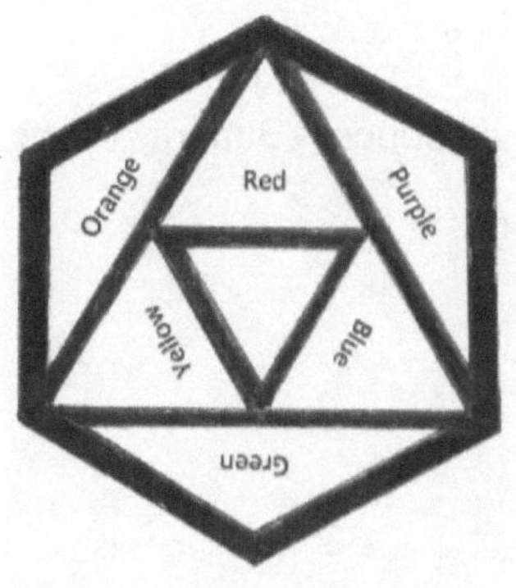

DAVID SUPPER

'This book is dedicated to my wife Bryony who has brought light into my life.'

Introduction to DAVID SUPPER's new volume of verse.

by COLIN WAKEFIELD

Author of The Rhyming History of England

It was a pleasure to be asked to write this short introduction to David Supper's new volume of poetry. You can tell immediately that David is an artist, for his poems are brimming with colour and visual imagery. The appropriately titled *Colours* evokes a dazzling picture of the world of butterflies – the eyes of the peacock "in iridescent greens and blues"; the "zig and zag" of the tortoiseshell; and the painted ladies that "flit from bud to buddleia" as they flirt, admiringly, "with the admiral", a most arresting image.

Many of the poems take us on a journey – through nature, through a season, or to a place – so by the end of *Colours* "the brittle winter comes", although we can be confident, from what we have already experienced, that the annual cycle will begin anew. Enjoy *The Moth*, "fragile and frivolous", and the barnacle-clad whales that "recall a wilder age" in *Whale Watching*.

This volume is a rich medley of nature, seasonal change and touching reminiscence. In *On the Edge* I loved the "onion memories of you" that "fade in the dim half-light that deadens thoughts". I especially liked the deliberately ponderous rhythm of *The Naming of Slugs*, and the spare, but graphic, intensity of *Treasure*. Most intriguing of all, to me, was *Bridget Riley Eyes*: do read it for yourself and see what you think!

If you enjoy this wonderful selection of David's verse as much as I did, you are in for a treat.

Foreword

As an artist I use colour all the time in my visual work. The poems presented here all use colour in some way or are based on colour or how the subject matter is affected by colour. There is no theme other than this and often the poems are a response, entirely, to something I have seen in the world around me, rather than a particular circumstance.

I grew up in Reading, Berkshire, although I now live in Nottingham, and during my college years I spent the summer recesses working as an assistant lock-keeper on the River Thames. This may explain my love of water and in particular rivers; the sea also holds a great attraction for me and I find it a constant source of inspiration.

My poetry is often a response to something I have seen in the world around me, rather than a particular circumstance. I hope you, the reader, will also respond in a similar manner when you read the poems in this book.

David Supper

December 2020

Contents

Colours

Each year I wait,
anticipate,
waiting for the first,
first colours of summer
that mean so much to me;
orange-tipped,
zircon blue
and brimstone from the fire

Scalloped wing
and lower down
behind, red-dotted under
to make the point.
To follow on
the zig and zag of tortoise shell,
black-bordered, and
the complicated pattern
of red and blue and yellow.

A fragile wing
powdery to the touch,
that stains the hands
of those that dare;
and peacock's eyes
in iridescent greens and blues,
mimicking the greater creature
that stalks the lawns,
the velvet grass
of country piles.

Its stately progress
contradicted
by painted ladies
who show disdain,
in red and orange cobwebs,
and flit from bud to buddleia
flirting with the admiral,
admire the uniform
of red and black and white.

And on occasion
a sombre brown,
frayed and full of care,
would wander in my garden;
its yellow eye
looking for a field or speckled wood
where it could fly,
close to the ground, and
in and out of sunlit clearings.

All year I wait in vain,
even for the humble white
in all disguises,
for none are come;
and like my empty heart,
the nettles at the garden's end
will not give forth new life,
whose leaves remain intact
until the brittle winter comes.

Gamboge

Starting pale, just off-white
and turns to cream,
through straw and beige
to names of flowers,
Daffodil and Primrose;
which lead to brighter,
fully saturated versions of
permanent and cadmium —
the heavy metal of the range.

The primary and heat of helios,
increases richness and the value
of the depth of chrome;
resin from Cambodia
and ochre from the earth,
gives raw sienna,
which, when tinted
travels to the bay of Naples —
and burnt becomes
a darker hue, and disappears
into another sector.

Adding black to see the tones
takes us to a mossy world
of mystery, and of places
where borders start to merge,
of hooker's olives and
the swamps of putrefaction;
there the light begins to fade,
far from the source ——
on the edges of the wheel.

9.25 am

Only this morning, through the leaded light
I watched a blackbird on the Pyracanthus.
He was close. I could have touched him,
reached out and stroked his head,

there were white flecks on his feathers,
bright eyes, wary, his body trembled;
he gobbled the red-orange berries, each one
held for a moment in his beak. Then gone.

Potter's Pink

Born deep in the earth, at first
a liquid, then bubbling surface-wards;
cooling amongst geysers, faithful, true,
yellow stones shine in clear volcanic pools.

Moulded by a master, a craftsman,
leached of its water, contained, contented:
back into fire where salt and cobalt
glaze into, and onto the surface.

The colour is frozen, held for eternity,
and inside, the water which nourishes
stems that are cut, a vase for a flower —
a pink, dianthus Maimonides.

Coloured Doors

Behind the red door I gnashed my teeth and cursed the world,
religion and hatred between peoples — the injustices of everyday
greed and violence.

Behind the green door I cursed my peers, those who were
cleverer,
more articulate, better-looking, more certain of themselves and
their own lives.

Behind the yellow door I hid myself and refused to look beyond
comfort and safety, or to think of others and their needs or pain,
their suffering.

Behind the blue door I slipped into a stupor where little else
entered my consciousness and I existed rather than
lived — in a fog.

Behind the black door I sank into a deep depression, a hole
out of which there was no escape, lost my reason for living,
committed suicide.

Behind the white door I found sanctuary and then hope for a
future without pain, fear and mental anguish — I started to
understand myself.

Whale Watching

Fog-bound and sand-banked we stop
Dead!
The high-pitched torture of screeching metal assaults our ears
As prop meets silica and twists beyond repair;
Juddering, the boat limps harbour-bound,
Defeated!

Sunburst-blue when we return to the whaling ground,
Where, diving deep, the mighty humpbacks
Play teasingly with our boat as if in friendly rivalry.
Flashes of white before they rise to our encouragement,
Barnacle clad, these leviathans of the deep
Recall a wilder age.

Fast-back as the sun sets, I sit and watch
Three whelsh plumes in princely fashion —
Their foaming bubbles dance and catch the light
Azure, tinged with yellow and pink
While darkness falls across a wider sea.

Hambledon

I remember many years ago,
I stood on the weir at Hambledon
Watching the water tumble
From the higher level down
Hearing the steady roar assaulting sound,
Round inside my head and round
And down the gallons charged
Green and turquoise with a smell of silt,
Brown and dappled in the light
Which slipped through gently waving trees
And played upon the backs of trout
Swimming up against the flow,
And hiding in the deep.

When the wind blew against the stream
Across the cut white horses leaped,
And were confused within my eye
With stately swans and cotton bud
Reflections of the clouds, and gulls
That floated, bobbing up and down,
On waves so large they disappeared
From sight from time to time.
I remember in my youth a gypsy girl,
Whose skin was brown and her lips so red;
Laughing, she led me to the water's edge
And we curled our toes, childlike, in the mud.

Epitaph

There are no poppies in the Negev
just a red stain on the land —

Now I stand alone in a desert
and wait for the hidden hand,

To provide the milk and the honey
and soil where the seed will grow,

Think of the horn of plenty,
the warmth of the wind and the glow,

Dream of the hills and the valleys
that I used to know so well;

The brush in the valley of treasure
hides moistness, I can tell,

And the crowns of the rose-pink hills
in that far off land of dreams,

And the dark-eyed beauty on horseback
was only a mirage it seems.

The milk-white sap of the poppy
is too dry to run anymore,

Unable to forget the heartache
of a stranger at the door.

The Moth

Humming-bird honeysuckle with a flutter of wings,
three bars on each over a flashing of yellow,
sipping the nectar sucktorially deep, in the heart
of the flower, softly and gently on the edge of decay —
fragile and frivolous. Some kind of plane
with untilted wings, lifting and flying,
looping and droning — high in the sky;
resting on old wood and fading from sight.

Most of your brothers fly only at night,
nightjar or moth-hunter, goat-sucking creature,
bedazzled and drawn to the point of destruction,
seeking new worlds beyond your horizons;
images of larva cocooned in your death,
and seeing the flame as you take your last breath.

Clouds

Cumulus rising high above the land,
Seen from above, form ancient kingdoms
Wreathed in mist, some Narnia or Middle-earth
Bathed in sunlit optical illusions.

Large cloud-mountains at forty thousand feet,
Tops blown, like wind-catching mounds of snow,
Into soft, sculptured anvils or ice-creamed wedges;
More Oldenburg than he will ever know.

Formations that writhe and twist, making and re-making
Giant pillars, columns to support the palaces of gods;
With cotton-puffs of smaller clouds, blown by lighter winds
That scurry round the foothills of invention.

Stretching out are yet more kingdoms —
Some full of light and joy, and others
Hidden in a Mordor-dread of dark and gloom,
With ancient heroes and half-imagined monsters,

That lurk in darkly-clouded caves.
And stories told of old mythologies,
Of battles fought and famous victories won,
Triumphant against overwhelming odds.

Yet all I see are rim-lit colours,
Brushed with a pale and golden light;
Naples yellow, pale peach, orange —
And towering castles in my mind.

The Bonfire

His pride would only let him use one match
So, with care, he made the preparations:

Some dried grass, sticks and logs in thickness
Of ascending order — each in its own neat pile.

He checked and double-checked, until satisfied —
And then again he checked the wind,

Allowing air beneath, to let the fire breathe
Was the secret of success, and the source of pride.

At last he struck the match
And watched the kindling burn,

The greedy flames, fanned by the wind,
Licked and twisted, turned and blackened;

And then in order of their girth
He placed the sticks and logs upon the fire

Until the fire was hot, and in its speed
Would burn dry logs, green sap and all.

He sat and watched the flames,
And listened to the different sounds

That different woods and leaves could make;
And as in all the other times, he wondered,

How he came to be alone
In this, the autumn of his years.

And in his eye some moistness formed
Caused, he would have said, by drifting smoke.

At length the light began to fade,
And fire died to soft grey ash,

As deep in thought he poked cadavers,
That fell and broke gold-vermillion.

Sunset

Looking out to sea I watched the colours of the sun
change from brilliant yellow, through chrome to fiery red.
I thought of life and death and all things I'd left undone,
of love, being born again and all that that could mean.
An old man in a faded coat and water in his eyes said:
'You will remember this when your life begins to change,
as your friends and all your family slip away'.

Standing side by side, we watched the crimson giant
sink a quarter and a half, threequarters and a whole,
sliding lower, lower … until swallowed by the clouds.
I turned to ask him what he meant, and found myself alone
against the darkening sky. And on the windswept cliff,
the colours of the grass began to fade into shades of night …
I shivered, zipped my coat and headed for the village lights.

Fetish

As I entered the room — I saw her at once
surrounded by men, vying for favours.
She laughed and she flirted in that way that she had
and swayed in her dress — all spangly and sparkly.
I looked at her feet with their nails painted red,
in her open-toed shoes all black and with gold,
at the curve of her leg and the shape of her ankle;
and I saw that her little toe
had curled over the edge,
of the sole of her shoe
and touched
        the
           floor.

Caversham

Walkways, pathways over gates,
weir way, weird way
seeking herons' rise.

Across the horseshoe,
where Kings haunt meadows
along the waterside.

In the deep, lie phantoms
of drowned Men —
sinking in mud's soft embrace.

And floods rise, in Winter's
watery sun a silver
stream — woven with red.

Blue skies cast lovers' shadows
and a shiver, a shudder
in that lonely, empty place.

The Naming of Slugs

In damp moist places,
under large flat stones,
hidden under rotting leaves,
lurking in the mossy carpet
at the bottom of the fence;
or beneath a broken pot
hiding from the sun,
waiting for the rain
living blindly in the dark,
leaving silvery trails,
slippery slimy revolting creatures,
cousin to the common snail —
no one would think of eating you!

Netted slug Deroceras reticulatum
exuding your thick and sticky milky slime;
Great grey slug Limax maximus
an eight-inch repugnant snake of a slug
eating your way through decay;
Budapest slug Milax budapestensis
dark grey with bright orange
lines along your back, muncher of roots,
destroyer of crops, pestilence!
Great black slug Arion ater
you sway from side to side,
gorging on rotting vegetation.

On the Edge

I am caught in this hard stony place
between yellow-grey lichen rocks,
in a no-man's land of grit and shale,
pock-marked and blasted, twisted wire
grabbing and tearing flesh into flags;
a narrow strip dividing a turquoise sea
and a desert reddened by conflict,
wind-blown ruins of another life.
My onion memories of you
fade in the dim half-light
that deadens thoughts,
grips my heart in sorrow,
stretches credulity beyond reason
staring hollow-eyed until time ends.

Triton square

A thousand windows looking down
blinded by the screech of light –
reflected souls, trapped in double glazing,
mirrored in the eyes of others,
imprisoned through no fault of theirs;
forced to watch and witness Man's creation.
Below sit huge black granite slabs
that line the edges of the square,
black pavoirs cordon off the flowerbeds
raised above the level paths,
where white cyclamen, wearing red-stained hearts
line up in regimental order,
their dark green leaves neatly pressed,
ready for inspection.
On the far side of the square,
caught by slanting light, stand twelve trees
in battle formation like heavy cavalry,
their leaves shining, shimmering,
in anticipation of the fight.
Even the grass, caught fast by blackened bricks,
undulates in waves, waiting for the trumpet blast.
The soft blanket of silence is interrupted only
by the whirling, dust-blown leaves,
browned and curled – fallen before their time.

Alice's Door

She opened the door to a bright light,
to the garden's profusion of colour.

The radiating petals of flowers
are bee-kissed; each one
like a paper sun; its hue
ringed and lit
by the warmth
of an earthly star,
high in a June sky.

What the light has breathed
into life and nurtured,
rain complements, thirsty roots
absorb water, make growth:
a cycle, as if
sun and rain know
the life force that they give.

And so she strains to see
through the tiny door,
wondering how she could enter
this paradise of nature;
as she cries
her tears start falling, trying
to forget her size, her humanity.

Looking through a window at the birth of the world

Everything begins at the dawn of time:
darkness is peeled back like old skin —
heat excites the elements of life
that lie trapped in pools between
newly formed rocks, still smouldering.
Froth flows full of magma and ash
Steam shrouds the view;
sulphur and chlorine are pungent
in the gas black choking air.
Light streams like gold
through gaps in the atmosphere;
lightning showers gleam against
the reds and ochres of a nascent sky.
Chemicals react in boiling water.
Something stirs below the window,
I polish my glasses and lean forward,
squinting, to see more clearly.

Treasure

A pearl sat on a leaf and waited:
a drop of dew, a perfect jewel.
Reflecting light from inside out
blue and white and
deep viridian green,
floating on a breath of wind.
Look closely, and you will see
yourself trapped inside this
globe; brush the leaf
to gain your freedom,
and destroy the moment.

Sonning

Crumbling and tumbling or falling,
me on my own, poling the gates —
brown strings swirling and
peering for hidden naiads;
sun glistens to star-burst light
of silt-green, mud-brown,
sluggish, lazy waters.

Weeds pulling, waving in eddies
wrapping round ankles — ending a life.
Lock paddles rise, rushing
and gushing down to the sea,
"I'll follow, I'll follow…"
teeming with wildlife
and wild, white-bloated faces.

Sonnet

You are lovelier than a summer's day,
Brighter than the sky above,
Stronger than the grass beneath my feet;
Your hair outshines the golden sun,
Your lips are redder than any rose I know,
Your tongue sweeter than a honey bee,
Your skin much paler than the moon
That twins its sister in the night.
When you curl your hand in mine and
place your head inside the hollow of my neck,
I feel your breath hot against my throat,
Your hair brushed velvet on my cheek,
Your heart beating just like mine,
Your face glowing, bathing me in love.

Gina 'C'

Taut, straining the knotted rope, tide at full flush,
halyards clink, a keen wind to squeal and wheel —
gulls in a blinding light off dancing water.
Dragon-flair, tattered, torn, bravely crying
independence, cheek by jowl, blue, red and
black-bottomed, kicking against harbour walls.
Sibling, two brothers slap each other hard
waiting as the tide rises, falls — an accolade.

Buildings crowd around and cluster on the cliff,
jostling for a better view, cream, yellow
blue and orange, green, grey; small figures
stare back, braced against the blow, paddling for crabs.
Love made no sense, hair tangled, skin scuffed
and lined, caught in the light of a setting sun.

Meet a Glass Darkly

The room has a low aspect
with planks of wood,
the blue-grey of an overcast sky,
a single window is shaded
where furry leaves of a fig tree
overlap and rub incessantly,
up and down, marking the glass
with a sticky residue.

Occasionally, when the wind has a mind,
the branches tap on the pane,
as if anxious to come in
and sit for a while by the fire.
In the grate, blackened
by years of use, embers glow dully,
pulsating … grey wisps of smoke curl lazily
round in a corkscrew, not anxious to escape.

Linoleum covers the floor
cracked, stained with sunspots,
shadows trace the walls
making them swell and quiver.
Dead flies lie on the window sill,
others rub their restless hairy feet,
zoom round and round,
singing, dancing, doomed to failure.

In a chair by the table,
a man sits in silent contemplation,

worn hands immobile on his lap,
barely breathing: he sees a young boy
nervously arrive at the door —
seeking sanctuary.

Rhossilly

Below the cliffs, white sand curves for more than a mile,
almost as far as the eye can see, sweeping all before,
wave upon wave of incoming tide reclaims the beach.
A lone figure, head down, battles wind and the snarl
of dragons' teeth, as he struggles to gain the cliff path —
rain-drops tear at skin, hard as bullets, ricochet to the ground.
Out at sea, barely visible, the Worm's Head surrenders to foam
and spray, the heavy weight of water seeking its destruction.

Wind-blown on the cliff top, steely grass, grey-green, bends
as if in a forge-glow. Twisted ribbons of seaweed in banks,
piled high, mermaids' purses, home for sand-thrips, flotsam, jetsam.
Thick rope lies half buried, wrenched from ships stripped bare
of safety, harbourless; hearts sink at the thought of lost loved ones,
hopes of a safe passage fade quickly as a wet moon at the
winter solstice.

On the shore, brave men, (some would say foolhardy), run to
the foaming edge and wetsuited, leap through waves half as high
again, of freeze-cold, blood-shattering, skin-stinging saltwater;
aim for the centre of deep turquoise-grey funnels, a perfect curve,
until crashing, crushed to the bottom — caught by a rip tide,
stumbling to try again, dragging on sand. The ocean swells
in a cove, rising and falling, tears like seawater are salty.

Changing Light

Light-tinged steam, blown from cooling towers,
ragged clouds catching rim-light from a hidden sun,
blue-patched sky in layers, palette knife spread
impasto, ridges edged with yellow and as time
passes, turn pink from light filtered through thick air.
In the wind, fully clothed trees sway and toss leaves
which catch light, flickering like tiny lighthouses —
transmitting warnings to the unwary.

Eyes bright as if light inhaled with each breath
shines forth in a glow that pulls me in to you,
helpless as a moth I flutter, unable to escape
I surrender to your embrace, your radiance;
your refulgence transforms me from dull brown
to glorious colour: dazzling, blinding, resplendent.

Reverie

If I glance from my screen to the window
I am presented with views of a red brick wall,
each brick is unique in colour and shape,
stained with orange and brown in a hundred ways.
I see nothing else, except in the corner, a triangle of sky.
I can't see the sun as it faces north-east,
but sometimes its light cascades down the bricks,
in the morning or later, in the afternoon.
My wall has a pipe half grey, half black,
that carries their sewage away, and just out of view
is a window of the bathroom next door,
the paint on the frame is brown and starting to peel,
the wood underneath is silvery-grey.
The blades of the air-vent spin this way and that
whirling, rotating, pushed by the wind.
Late at night, when the light comes on
and the people next door make ready for bed,
I can see shadowy figures brushing their teeth —
I drop down the blind to shut me away,
alone in my room my thoughts are my own,
to imagine a way through the rest of my life,
cocooned and protected from the world outside.

Through a gate in Avalon

On a hidden path
lit by a glowing lamp,
enclosed by low branches —
the rustling of leaves.
Blue and red of hydrangeas
and deep viridian
of shiny camellias,
cyclamen hiding beneath —
white against green.
A holly, hard against
the elephantine trunk
of a copper beech,
prickling, protecting.
Yews, either side,
guarding the entrance,
the curve of the door
roses in glass
stipple and frosted.
Warm on the inside —
a frosty reception
for boots worn with walking
and covered in mud.
Where mountains are broken
and lakes are unswum,
the water comes tumbling
reviving, refreshing
forming islands of green.
Long strands of grass
are tossed by the wind,

clouds scudding by
are suddenly stranded:
when quiet is called for
and Nature must sleep.

Lament

For me your dying was difficult
and I shall not soon forget
the way you lay there at the end
yellow skin blotched purple

you went without a fight
breathing shallow, out went a light
not a tremor could I see
playing on the surface of your skin

your hair turned yellow too
the sunken cheeks
as if you had drawn one last breath
and then you slept, peacefully

you lay on yellow sheets
stained with juices from your life
did you consentingly let go
or had your mind already taken flight?

Cloughie

Standing close-by Market square,
a bronze with hands clasped held aloft,
mounted on a plinth of cold grey granite,
he stares on all with baleful eyes
and rheumy nose, that once was red
for taking more, so they say,
of his fair share of liquid gold.
But his achievements far outshine
the sheen of bronze that covers him,
that all who see, forgive the weakness
of the man who brought such glory,
golden days to Forest and the Rams;
fitting that he should now forever stand
between the King, the Queen and Fothergill.
All who come to pay him homage,
are reminded of his sense of joy and iron will.

The Man Whose Coat was Far Too Big

Shrivelled like a prune, the weathered face
poked out from beneath acres of black gabardine,
a trench coat, belted and of vast proportions;
the puce coloured scarf caught fast around his neck
was like a wound, a gaping hole or some exotic
fruit, gashed purple contrasting with its sombre outer skin.
His nose, sprouting hair that echoed his moustache —
pale and sandy shades of grey, wobbled all the time
he talked, while his slender hands, the skin scabrous
like dried leaves, scrabbled with his man-bag,
searching for a Blackberry phone and multi-tasking,
he read his messages, text replies, all without pausing.
Beneath the voluminous outer covering,
his feet protruded wearing black socks,
blue jeans and brand-new Nike trainers.

from the blue

black bird, yellow beak in winter
searching for food under dead leaves,
hopping lawns, pausing, listening;
red breast, brown bonnet
perches close-by, waiting
to grab unwary worms;
fat grey wood pigeon bounces,
sways on thin branch always in pairs;
throats swell, feathers puffed,
sounds warble, echo, bouncing off trees;
colourless bag of bones, skin stretched
over skull, narrow bitter lips,
speech clipped, hopeless in love,
lonely in old age, rails at boisterous
young, careless of the world,
wheels turn, time moves on,
remembered by no man or beast;
birds fly, flock and wheel,
nest for generations,
metamorphose to fossils,
layered, buried, geologically.

The Camellia changes Beds

Tall as a small tree, its pink flowers lie squashed,
rotting on the ground signalling the end of spring,
new growth emerges from leaf axils, lime-fresh
green vibrantly contrasting with deep, waxy viridian.

For two days I had been carefully digging a trench,
circular, gradually working my way underneath
the massive root-ball. Out of the hole came lumps
of brick, coke, glass and pottery, Victorian detritus.

The neck of a bottle, green-glazed tiles, a fragment
of blue delft plate, the curve of a cream-ware jug,
complete with part of its handle, a broken lid
from a long lost teapot and half a white saucer.

Carefully cutting roots to free it from the ground,
we heaved the bush onto an ancient wheel-barrow,
dragged it unwillingly through the wooden gate
into the back garden, towards a new hole, freshly dug.

Wildly swinging back and forth, resisting our efforts
to get it to stand upright, it suddenly capitulated
and slipped home, while we frantically piled earth
stamping it down to secure its position, before letting go.

By the time I had got the hose and soaked the
compost round the base, the new green growth
had flopped worryingly. A further soaking
did nothing to allay our fears — only time will tell.

Scheduled for felling, we had offered a last chance
of life to this extraordinary plant in a new position —
it was not to be in our fading memory, but here
in the roaring daylight, with the wind and the rain

in its branches and on its leaves, a wild cacophony
of living in the burnished glow of the morning sun.

Harvest Moon

A purple sky
complements
yellow
ripening corn
waving
in the wind
the sun
and the moon
opposites
at each end
of the field.

Rain falls
fiercely
blowing
corn dollies'
skirts
inside out
paedophiles leer
salivate
under a dirty
blood-red
moon.

Desire

She had a sparkling jewel in her navel,
which glinted in the late October sunshine,
her midriff, splotchily tanned, flat and firm;
my eyes were glued to this expanse of flesh,
a young girl, unaware of her sensuality
chewed gum vigorously, her dyed blonde hair
piled like a thatch on her head, red lips, blue eyes.
The jewel moved, rotated as she walked,
at once green, then blue —
I wondered how the hot needle
had pierced her skin,
a splash of red, another jewel,
life's force hovering
before being wiped away.
Desire churned my stomach.
I wanted to say something,
but her youth, the way her teeth
tore at the gum, her open mouth,
the movement of her jaw
forced me to stay silent.
From the bus I saw her meet up
with three identikit mates,
blonde cows chewing the cud,
pavements stripped bare of grass.

Losing Sight

When all is lost in the dimmest light
and clarity fails as shapes blur
into tones of grey, and the world darkens
month by month; from a shining star
to a pinprick of light, like a quick fade
on the silver screen, a mist covers
your pale green eyes, searching my face
for answers to questions never asked.

There must you remain, unseeing,
unsighted, blinkered, invisible;
while you walk in dazzled darkness
colours do not fade, flowers' bright
profusion of blooms will remain:
imprinted on your heart, your memory.

In each house in the street,

in each street in the town,
in each town in the land,
we live our lives on standby
red and green, blinking,
flickering lights in every room —
an electronic eye, burns,
pricks at our conscience.

Everyone is guilty, you (and I)
and all of us ignore the obvious,
if we're to keep our green, pleasant
land, our planet blue,
floating in the milky way,
home for future generations,
we must stop the CO_2.

Reduce our energy consumption,
consider all the other options
or we'll leave a wasted land,
where little grows but weeds and tears:
mutants scurry in the undergrowth,
mud flowers lace the ground,
their scent, fragrant as wet compost.

Apotheosis

When I close my eyes, in the pinkness
that is the obverse of my eyelids
are two tiny black spots
like a tear in my existence —
not big enough to slip through —
but black, dark as night, dark as velvet.

Like a tear in the universe, a rip
in the spacetime continuum —
slipping through to another dimension
where the light of two suns
is caught in a mirror, filling my eyes,
my mind, with a blinding flash

of pale, golden yellow: pinpoints of molten orange.

Late Arrival

March is hunched,
threaded, almost over
and daffodils still refuse
to show their yellow,
nodding heads.
Snowdrops carpet
the woodland
behind the house,
their white petals,
en masse, echo
the recent snowfall.
Crocuses warm themselves
in the weak sunshine,
opening to
reveal their
saffron hearts.
Spring limps lamely
into the garden.

Spring

On my rockery wild violets grow,
snowdrops bow their heads in a final dance,
now spring is sprung the primrose smiles
as it feels the warmth from the sun above.

There, where the Aubretia's purple petals
spill over soft moss-covered Mansfield stone,
I'd lay you down amongst the bluebells,
lay you down with blossoms in your hair.

Where Muscari blooms and Ranunculus'
star-shaped flowers, bright against dark red leaves
and Euphorbia's multi-coloured bracts,
rich purple-red, like a vintage ruby port.

If I close my eyes I can see a young girl,
carefree, dancing naked across the lawn,
tip-toeing on stepping stones like giant lily pads,
her long blonde hair shining in the sunlight.

Her laughter, yours, rings round the garden
like the peal of a thousand tiny Canterbury bells,
that toll their knell for our lost youth, the days
when we had no thoughts of how life would end.

The rusting, rustling leaves of Montbretia,
lie bent and twisted in amongst the dry crackle
of fallen beech leaves, while we, with streaming eyes
see the sudden onset of our own autumnal days.

Butterfly

When skin splits and from a grubby shell
fragility emerges, quivering, bedraggled,
a drying, stretching wing-forming moment,
a wonder of colour; barely daring to blink
I watch the transformation, the metamorphosis
from dull brown to a light-dazzling shimmer.
Then comes a moment when I know
this creature, in its magnificence, will take to the air,
free of earthly ties, to dance on the wind,
feel the sun and its life-giving warmth,
to live for a day, that brief moment in time
before the sun sets, and in the darkness
the dust that once was a living being,
scatters amongst the grasses, an ending,
a dying, mourned by no-one but I.

In the Garden

The lawn, newly laid,
has that unkempt look
like hair freshly washed
and towelled dry, tousled
and in need of a stiff brushing.

Somehow the greenness
looks artificial, and the lines
between turfs bend imperceptibly,
as if blown by the wind
or in a choppy Sargasso Sea.

When I looked you were already
on it, walking in high heels,
spiking the grass, sinking in its lushness,
claiming you for its own
as you struggled to remain upright.

You stood alone in the afternoon sun,
your shadow slanting viridian,
your pale skin already turning to stone.

Autumn

The ivy grows heavy, flowering on the wooden fence
separating me from the outside world. Green-gold florets

cluster in the late October sunshine, a rich, sickly perfume
sucks in an army of insects to the last chance saloon.

A regiment of admirals gorge themselves, snorting lines
of nectar, smartly dressed in freshly ironed uniforms;

occasionally a marauding bee skirmishes, before retreating
in the face of overwhelming odds — there is plenty for all.

The grass is mown for the last time and close-by, the sun
kissing her shoulder, stands Pandora, winter jasmine

curling around her ankles; her box tightly shut. The ivy
holds on with fibrous tendrils waiting for winter's blast.

How much does it take?

Four days of heavy frost, a startling cold
fills my lungs, my breath hangs
as a heavy cloud, blown by a chill, seeping wind.

The world has changed: last week's snow,
frozen into ice, hangs rigidly from pale rooftops,
refracting light from a weak winter sun.

All is covered in a delicate lace,
even the obstinate leaves that rattle on twigs,
iron gates, barbed wire, open fields and hills.

My hand, grown brown as leather,
finds frozen blooms of the dog rose, pale red,
a flash of warmth in shrivelled undergrowth.

The air has changed colour,
it hovers like a fog, glistens like ivory:
I try breathing through a white mouth.

Belladonna

There is something exotic about perfume,
the way it hangs in the air in the space
where you were, just a moment ago,
it lingers, inflames the delicate tissues
of sensory glands, intoxicates, deadly.

Through shades of night, I follow the trail
that you leave, mesmerised by the scent
and rustle of silk of your purple dress,
layered like petals of a dangerous flower:
succumb to the fragrance of a certain death.

What becomes of us?

One day all seems serene,
so far the journey's been quite smooth,
then the next it all begins to crumble:
each breath more laboured than the last,
it casts a shadow on our own mortality,
days blur as if viewed through frosted glass.

The sun still hangs yellow in the sky,
rain-washed streets clear the tired dust,
new snowfall, clean, white, refreshes
grey winter landscapes, there is injustice in the air;
a warm flurry of blood in the pulse
that surprises the brain with a moist kiss.

Feel for the shape of disturbed waters,
concentric rings expanding, fading,
dark years of the future remain hidden, unknown;
for the present heaven is to be found on earth,
think of flowers in wild fields, blue skies,
the balm of warm winds caressing a May morning.

Storm over the Brisbane River

The sultry heavy air lies softly, suffocating;
hazy tops of hills blur and merge with a dark sky,
in the warm firm wind, leaves blow like streamers
at a Chinese festival, rustling expectantly,
suddenly escaping, one bid for freedom
before diving to join the tinder-dry undergrowth.

Lilac flowers ripped from the Jacaranda tree
splodge the ground, indigo stains,
to match deepening purple across the valley;
peeling bark from Eucalypts, soft to the touch,
like parchment, striated, light greys give way
to pale golden browns, lie strewn on the ground.

At the Crossings, where the river widens, bends,
caught in a sudden shaft of sunlight,
a black and white heron flaps lazily,
gliding low over the muddy tidal river;
from the graph of a dead branch, a small bird
dives, returns, then dives again — over and over

A lone black swan buffeted by waves,
drifts with the current, blown downstream
and out of sight; a white duck nestles
at the foot of a stunted pine, feathers ruffled,
its blood-red face peering, waiting;
raucous crows wheel, screaming warnings.

Flights of butcherbirds form angry squadrons,
screeching, darting this way and that in perfect formation
as the black threatening clouds gather themselves
release a torrent of rain, and flashes of lightening
accompanied by low rumbles of thunder;
soon the sticky heat, returns, deadening sound and spirit.

Keeping Calm

In the middle of an anguished search
when a storm wrenched mind from reason
and the peace that beckons seems ever more attractive;
suddenly she is there, hair brushed into cute blonde curls,
pink lipstick, a crazy laugh that brooks no contradictions.

Amidst the red and black tiles, empty walls,
brown polished floorboards, she takes you in
and when you touch, a shiver;
her eyes cover every inch of your face,
flicker, as she measures your effect on her.

The kiss, when it comes, scatters pink light
with a sound of breaking, your stomach lurches,
waves drown each motion, each thought
as you lie in the darkened room, half in, half out
of dreamland, while your bodies wait to become lovers.

In the morning a sudden sun dazzles, confuses,
in panic you turn to the bed, tears like warm rain
on your cheeks, but she is still there
smiling in her sleep, her hand outstretched,
the blue veins traced like solid marble.

Bridget Riley Eyes

I press my fingers to my eyes, where,
to my surprise, I find I have Bridget Riley eyes.
The geometric shapes evolve, revolve,
then turn upon themselves to give,
in black and white, my Bridget Riley eyes.
Think of this mattress as a boat, afloat
upon a sea of dreams where gentle waves
rock us back and forth. To breathe,
you snatch so neatly at the air and drift
in a bright tabasco sky. Each memory
hesitates before it steals, silent as the night,
and then returns my Bridget Riley eyes.

Bridgford Lock

Sure-footed ducks strut the slippery concrete apron,
a loose feather floats lazily on the surface,
hovers on the lip of a man-made waterfall,
before being sucked into a maelstrom
of water, crashing down to the lower level.

Two cream and white swans ruffle their feathers
in the wind, preen fastidiously in the hope of a chance meeting.
Upstream the sun glances blindingly off textured water,
while timid moorhens hide beneath leaf-stripped
skeletal branches of a winter weeping willow.

Dog-walkers worry their pets, shout for them to behave
while collecting small parcels in black plastic bags.
Duckweed, so plentiful a few weeks ago,
is now nowhere to be seen, brambles lie broken
and twisted, even the rushes have retreated into clumps.

From shopping trolleys blue mats are taken
and laid out on the damp seat as the sun makes a weak
effort to convince us that the worst is now over.
Children, in red macs, squeal as they plough through puddles
on aluminium scooters, oblivious to time passing.

On the Beach

Across a windswept beach with clouds scudding
a dark autumnal sky, it was not exactly raining
but the air was thick, cold and damp.
The sea an infinite pavement of grey sludge,
a dull green slime oozed around the rock pools,
in a rough night the sea had dumped piles of bladderwrack
in a thick continuous scum at the foot of the cliff face.
A man shivers, pulls his coat tighter and bends into the wind,
he whistles for his dog, who races over, depositing
in front of his master, a severed human hand.
Ribbons of flesh curl from well chewed fingers,
white bones protrude from a shredded glove
of black muslin, grasping at the empty air.
The man shudders and retches his breakfast
onto the ribbed sand; gulping, he clips the lead onto the dog's
collar and half walks, half runs to the promenade,
stumbling up the steps to the nearest telephone.

Snowfall

Soft flakes fall from a lead-grey sky,
black figures stumbling, flattening,
flattened under the white of the day;
a redwing perches on a cotoneaster tree,
gobbling berries till the tree's stripped bare,
mottled white feathers on neck and breast
a white mascara around its eyes.

In darkness, pierced with a passion,
the groom seeks his lost bride:
there as a badge of courage or a medal
just now, from the frosted branches
a blush of crimson, seeping, staining,
scarlet berries, red from a heart
that was broken, long ago.

Untitled

Brown, brittle eucalyptus leaves
spiral in the wolf-wind, float forlornly
to the greening pool surface
that I cleared only yesterday.

Green and fresh palm fronds toss wildly,
while below, dried carcasses split, pull
and leave a smooth sheen, a condom trunk,
each year marked, scarred, ring-bound.

A myriad of insects struggle to survive
on the meniscus of a chlorine soup,
while ducks, not fussy, crap green slime
on white slabs, in turquoise water.

The house, perched on stumps, shivers,
shakes, each gust louder than the last,
air forced through every gap
whistles, moans, like a discontented banshee.

The Forage

Each year the gathering of fruits from hedgerows
Becomes a ritual that marks the coming of the equinox,
To a chorus of pigeons, doves and raucous screeches of crows,
The forage brigade stand with plastic bags, fingers stained purple,
And dream of bubbling saucepans of jams, syrups and jellies.

A bold squirrel grabs a newly-fallen walnut in its mouth
And makes off, the nut, larger than its head, clamped firmly in its jaws.
Its brothers and cousins make a messy meal of unripe hazelnuts,
Elderberries hang their heads, heavy with black fruits,
Wild rose hips, red with promise, dangle just out of reach.

This is the season of acorns, from which mighty trees will grow,
And in the hedges Columbine winds its tendrils, climbing higher,
Ever higher, its driven white trumpets blow a silent fanfare
To herald the approach of Autumn; another year turns
Towards winter, as time slips by, almost unnoticed.

December 21st

Curled round the fire, wrapped in a blanket
fingers and toes still freezing, outside,
the crisp, white frost shatters tender stems
of plants — in nature's cruel divide.

The bright sun slants through the window
catching speckled dust in its rays,
last night's snow tries hard to melt —
but turns to ice in these bitter winter days.

Distant black clouds rush on the wind,
bringing night midway to the afternoon,
then in fury, blow — whitening the ground;
lights glow orange, mocking the sun too soon.

Shivering indoors, only four days to go —
while we are warm inside, let it snow!

Island

In a month or so
the trees will begin
to lose their leaves,
already those of the
horse chestnut
look brown and tired.

Crowded together,
or huddled
in mid-stream,
now the deep green
of late summer —
spring long forgotten.

A superstructure
in viridian,
full and heavy,
one tall mast
navigating the current
against the wind.

The long prow
protrudes horizontally,
dragon-like,
its stiff legs
search for a footing
in the soft mud.

White feathers drift
this way and that:
swans' down surrenders
up its message,
slaps against faces
too young to know.

Thames Memories

Silt in grey-green water
the scent of mud, pock-marked
by cow hooves
in water meadows,
that slope on either side.
Bright blue damsel flies
flit here, there, laying eggs
below the surface.
The schlock of water slapping
banks as a boat rides by,
the vee of waves,
frilled edges like the comma
and small tortoiseshell.
Picnics in the long soft grass,
poohsticks under bridges,
ice-creams from the lock-side shop,
black and yellow caterpillars
swarming on ragwort.
Long days, lazy days —
we dawdle on the towpath,
reluctant to go home.

Ambience

The tarmac path winds its way,
A black ribbon in a narrow wedge of green,
Which forces houses far apart.
Old railway sleepers form bridges across a stream
That purls inexorably towards the canal
A relic of a long, distant, industrial past.
Beneath, the water flows and struggles
Over plastic bottles, cans, foil wraps et al,
And here a section of broken fence
Makes a lower crossing between
The steep sides, guarded by nettles and brambles
That send thick, thorny spikes high into the air,
And make a barrier for the unwary explorer.
Amongst the tree are bricks, tiles, lumps of concrete,
A burnt mattress or two and beneath the water,
A ghostly blue bicycle raises a pedal as if to say,
'Help me, I'm here, pull me out. Please!
Release me from this man-made swamp,
I still have many miles to roam.'

Spumes of May reach for the sky
The Dog Rose' delicate flowers
Pure white below to a blush of pink above,
Wild cherries form amongst the leaves
From red to black, sour to sweet.
Rosa rugosa, an escapee from its garden prison,
Blooms in hedgerows wild and free,
Creamy pancakes of elderberry blossom
Spring into view at every turn and hide

A shopping trolley which lies drunkenly,
Half buried in the undergrowth;
A plastic ride-on scooter, broken in two,
A brown withered pine from Christmas last
And a squashed, discarded traffic cone,
The metal cover atop an artificial hillock
Hints at access to a malodorous sewage pipe.
Despite Man's best efforts to contaminate,
This detritus slowly disappears
As Nature covers all, with a soft, verdant carpet.

Tenby

In the evening sunshine colours glow
with the promise of an early summer.

I awake to a dense sea-mist, shrouding boats
in the harbour with a ghost-like charm.

I can hear the whisper of the tide as it creeps
across the sand, gripping hulls waiting to float.

We shiver by the fire in Planties' lower bar
sipping lukewarm beer, the best Wales can offer.

For two days the mist holds the town in a cold grip —
on my last day the sun shines mockingly bright,

Diamonds twinkle on a high tide of blue surfaces,
striped umbrellas open like the flowers of a rock-rose.

Herring gulls wheel in the air, screeching
as they land, sharp beaks ripping at plastic bags

Waiting to be collected, scattering contents
across picture postcard views, demanding to be fed.

St Lucia

Clouds form and disappear,
the beach shape-shifts
from day to day.
A nut rolls up the sand
chased by effervescent foam;
yellow sand-crabs,
black eyes on stalks,
scramble sideways
hole to hole.
Red-flagged
foolhardy swimmers
plunge headfirst into breakers,
a sporting chance, in extremis.

Some bubble wrap
amongst the spume,
drapes itself around a rock,
glistening like silver sea-weed;
black oil tubes coil themselves,
snake-like, waiting to strike
unwary beach-combers.

In the space between
sky and sea,
the sun sets
an angry red.